W9-ANG-144

American Bison

Arthur Best

New York

Published in 2019 by Cavendish Square Publishing, LLC
243 5th Avenue, Suite 136, New York, NY 10016

Library of Congress Cataloging-in-Publication Data

Names: Best, B. J., 1976- author.
Title: American bison / Arthur Best.
Description: First edition. | New York : Cavendish Square, 2019. |
Series: Migrating animals | Includes index.
Identifiers: LCCN 2017048040 (print) | LCCN 2017049628 (ebook) | ISBN 9781502637055 (library bound) |
ISBN 9781502637079 (paperback) | ISBN 9781502637086 (6 pack) | ISBN 9781502637062 (ebook)
Subjects: LCSH: American bison--Migration--Juvenile literature. | Animal migration--Juvenile literature.
Classification: LCC QL737.U53 (ebook) | LCC QL737.U53 B49 2019 (print) | DDC 599.64/3--dc23
LC record available at https://lccn.loc.gov/2017048040

Editorial Director: David McNamara
Copy Editor: Nathan Heidelberger
Associate Art Director: Amy Greenan
Designer: Megan Metté
Production Coordinator: Karol Szymczuk
Photo Research: J8 Media

Printed in the United States of America

Contents

American bison are big.

They are brown.

They are also called **buffalo**.

5

Some bison live on farms.

Some bison live in zoos.

Some bison live in the wild.

Bison eat a lot of grass.

They drink a lot of water.

9

Bison can live by **mountains**.

They live high up.

There is grass.

There is water.

11

It gets colder in **autumn**.

It starts to snow.

The grass dies.

The bison can't eat it.

The bison move lower down.

It will be **warmer**.

There will be grass to eat.

There will be water to drink.

It snows more.

Bison move to find food.

They move to find water.

17

The snow melts in spring.

Grass grows.

Bison like to eat new grass.

19

It gets warmer.

The bison go **higher** up.

They live by a mountain again.

They will be there all summer!

21

New Words

autumn (AW-tum) One of the four seasons; also called fall.

buffalo (BUHF-uh-loh) Bison.

higher (HI-er) Above a thing.

mountains (MOUN-tenz) Huge hills of rock.

warmer (WARM-er) Not as cold.

Index

About the Author

Arthur Best lives in Wisconsin with his wife and son. He has written many other books for children. Once in South Dakota, a bison walked in front of his car.

About

Bookworms help independent readers gain reading confidence through high-frequency words, simple sentences, and strong picture/text support. Each book explores a concept that helps children relate what they read to the world they live in.